Everything You Need to Know About the Rise and Fall of the Roman Empire In One Fat Book

Ancient History Books for Kids

Children's Ancient History

BABY PROFESSOR

EDUCATION KIDS

Speedy Publishing LLC

40 E. Main St. #1156

Newark, DE 19711

www.speedypublishing.com

Copyright 2017

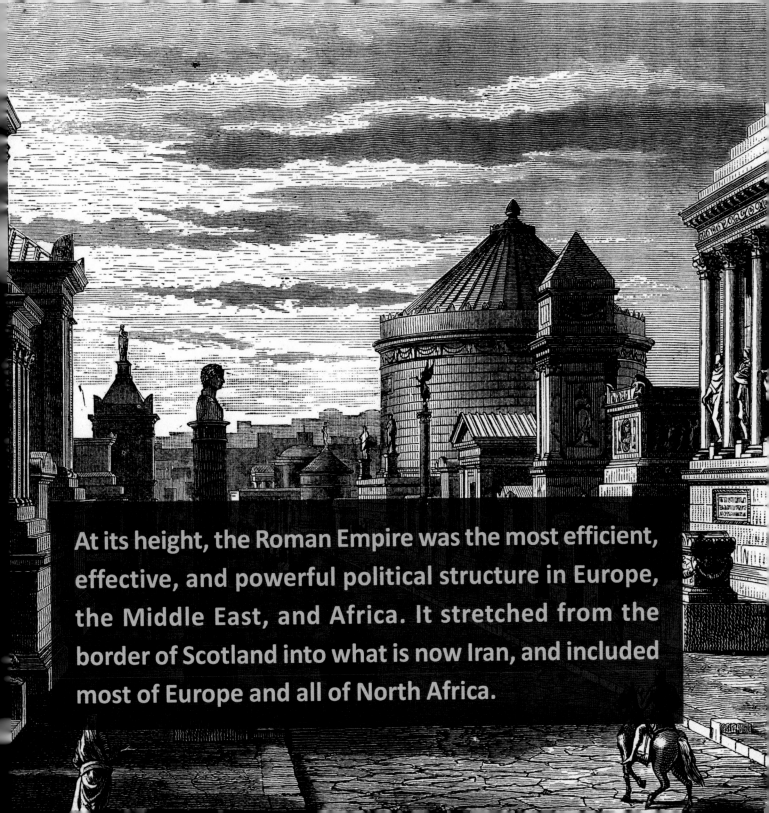

At its height, the Roman Empire was the most efficient, effective, and powerful political structure in Europe, the Middle East, and Africa. It stretched from the border of Scotland into what is now Iran, and included most of Europe and all of North Africa.

But how did it get to that success? And how did it end? Read on and find out!

Roman Forum

Fori Imperiali ruins

IN THE BEGINNING

The great Roman Empire started from a little village in central Italy, which was founded around 765 BCE. Roman tradition says it was founded by the twins Romulus and Remus, descended from heroes who fled the city of Troy after the Greeks destroyed it in the Trojan War. There is no historical support for this myth.

At first Rome had a king as its head. But after seven kings, the people of Rome developed a system of government called a "republic", which comes from the Latin words for "public matters". The highest authority in the Roman Republic was the Senate, a gathering of senior and influential men. The Senate would appoint officers for the army and people to head all the public offices.

ROMAN REPUBLIC

The Republic was successful, and continued for almost 500 years. Rome gradually expanded, absorbing neighboring tribes and villages. Sometimes this was peaceful, but sometimes Rome had to fight hard to overcome other strong civilizations, like the Etruscans and the Greeks.

The Republic's greatest rival was Carthage, a city on the coast of North Africa. Carthage and Rome fought over control of territories and trade routes, and Rome finally defeated and destroyed Carthage in 146 BCE.

Carthago

THE ROMAN WAY

There were four general classes in Roman society. At the top were the nobles. They were rich, powerful families, and usually provided the members of the Senate and the top generals of the army. They held most of the power in Rome, as well as most of the wealth.

The equestrian class, or the knights, were next. They were rich, but not noble. They would ride to war on horses, rather than marching.

Roman Salute

The plebeian class were free people, and included merchants, shop-keepers, builders, and other hard-working people. They usually had no power, but sometimes combined behind the tribunes, their elected leaders, to force changes from the Senate.

At the bottom of the pile were the slaves. They had no rights and could not own property, but many of them were highly skilled and worked as doctors, teachers, and accountants. Slaves were Romans who were so poor they sold themselves to clear their debts, and citizens of counquered countries and nations.

If you were a Roman citizen you had special rights that were not available to even powerful people who came from other countries.

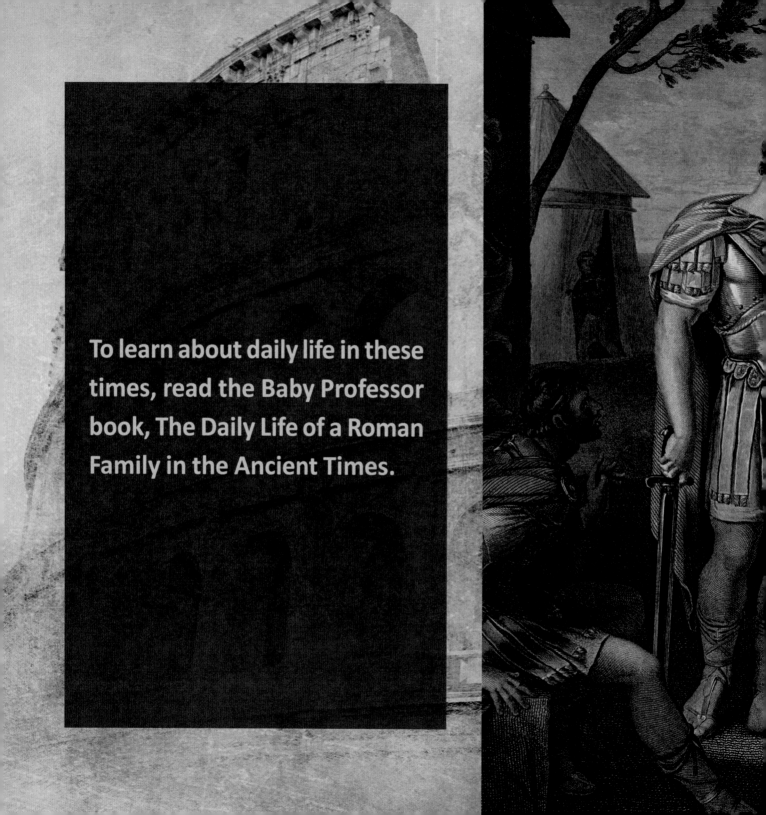

To learn about daily life in these times, read the Baby Professor book, The Daily Life of a Roman Family in the Ancient Times.

Roman Colosseum

Both republic and empire had success because the Romans had great armies and great organization. The armies were better organized and trained than those of their enemies, and usually had good generals to lead them. Rome built roads all across its territory so the armies could move quickly to deal with attacks or rebellions, and to let trade flow well. Huge aqueducts brought water over long distances to the cities. The government organized regular supplies of food basics so even the poorest citizens would have food; and they organized huge games and entertainments to distract people from their troubles.

REPUBLIC TO EMPIRE

As Rome expanded, it often faced crises and sometimes civil war. The Republic would raise up a temporary strong leader, but there was always a fear that he would try to become king. A series of strong leaders led to the struggle for supreme power between Pompey and Julius Caesar. This ended with both Caesar and Pompey dead, and the Republic in the hands of leaders who were king in all but name. They took the title Caesar after Julius Caesar; many were from his family, but as the years went by many Caesars were raised up because of their success as generals.

THE GREAT EMPERORS

The great empire usually had an emperor at its head, and sometimes two or three! Here are some of the most famous Roman Emperors.

JULIUS CAESAR

Julius Caesar was one of Rome's greatest generals, the conqueror of Gaul and the first Roman to lead an army into Britain. He was never the emperor, but members of the Senate killed him because they were afraid he was going to proclaim himself king. This lead to a struggle of several years that marked the end of the Republic and the start of the Empire.

AUGUSTUS

Augustus was Caesar's adopted son. He rose to power working with, and then fighting with, rivals like Marc Antony. He was the first formal emperor of the Empire. Under Augustus, the Empire expanded greatly into North Africa, Germany, and the Middle East.

CALIGULA

Caligula was a self-indulgent, erratic man who was convinced he had become a god. His reign almost brought down the Empire, and he was killed by his own soldiers.

CLAUDIUS

Claudius improved the organization of the Empire, and under him Roman armies won victories on many fronts. Under Claudius Rome conquered Britain. He was responsible for acqueducts and was a patron of literature.

NERO

Nero, like Caligula, was probably insane. He murdered his own mother and wife, and sent many Christians to death in the arenas to amuse the crowds.

TITUS

Before Titus became emperor he was a governor and general, He put down the revolt in Judea that ended the last independent Jewish state before the 20th century.

TRAJAN

Trajan, who ruled around 100 CE, was an effective administrator and war leader. Under him the empire expanded to its largest size, adding territory in northern Europe and in the Middle East.

HADRIAN

Hadrian was a highly-competent ruler. He concluded that the Empire had grown too large, and the armies were stretched too thin to defend it. He established the Rhine River as the northern frontier of the Empire, and built a wall near where the border is between Scotland and England to mark the edge of the Empire in Britain. He refocused Roman forces to face significant challenges from the Partians, and other forces in Asia.

DIOCLETIAN

A cavalry officer who rose through the ranks, Diocletian was proclaimed emperor around 284 after the death of the Emperor Carus, who was leading the army against Persia. Diocletan divided the empire into eastern and western halves, and established co-emperors to rule them. Diocletian was the 51st emperor of Rome, so you can see we have skipped over a lot of them!

CONSTANTINE

Under Constantine, Christianity, which had been illegal, became recognized as the religion of the Empire. Constantine set the capital of the eastern empire in Byzantium, which he renamed Constantinople. Learn more about the eastern empire in the Baby Professor book, The Byzantine Empire.

ROMULUS AUGUSTUS

Romulus Augustus was the very last emperor of the Roman Empire in the west. He was proclaimed at the command of his father, who was head of the imperial cavalry, and Romulus was little more than a figurehead for his father. He was a teenager, and was emperor for about a year in 475-6 CE before a soldier, Odoacer, overthrew him and proclaimed himself king of Rome.

THE END OF THE ROMAN EMPIRE

The Roman Empire collapsed under pressure from the outside, and because its internal parts were often at war with each other. Migrating tribes numbering millions of people from northern Europe and central Asia, themselves pushed along by forces in eastern Asia, overwhelmed Roman provinces and armies one by one. The Goths, Visigoths, Vandals, and Huns at first swept through Roman territory, looting and killing. But soon they were putting down roots and making their own home of what had been Roman provinces for hundreds of years.

As early as the time of Diocletian, Rome was having trouble finding enough men to fill the ranks of its legions. It started hiring "barbarian" fighters. These fighters were very competent and fierce, but they had little loyalty to the Empire. Many disruptions of power were caused by non-Romans who had learned their military skills within the ranks of the Roman legions.

Rome itself, and the cities of Italy, depended on shipments of grain from North Africa and tax revenue from the Near East. As these areas slipped out of Roman control, it became impossible to maintain the army the Empire needed, and the end came over the course of a very few years. The first big incursion by the Goths and others was in 376. The Roman frontier contracted, sometimes slowly, and sometimes like a landslide, and within 100 years the empire was no more.

LEARN MORE ABOUT ROME!

Rome lasted as a Republic for 500 years, and as an Empire for 600 more. The eastern part of the empire continued for another thousand years. There is much more to learn about Rome, Romans, other peoples of the period, and the influence of this great culture. Read Baby Professor books like Who Were the Barbarians? to learn more!

Visit

BABY PROFESSOR
EDUCATION KIDS

www.BabyProfessorBooks.com

to download Free Baby Professor eBooks
and view our catalog of new and exciting
Children's Books

Made in the USA
Monee, IL
30 September 2021